To my beloved mother, Diana Mallak, father, Emad Abou Fakher, and sister, Yara Abou Fakher, for all the unconditional love and long years of involuntary separation; the family of Ann Hoste, Joannes, Martha, Helene, and Jozef Vandermeulen for warmly welcoming me into their home; my friends, for all the ups and downs and everlasting memories; all the people who had to leave their homes and start new lives; and Stella, for her lifelong love.

—B. A. F.

To all the innocent victims of war

—D. B.

To Rano, my baby boy, without whose regular protests at bedtime and sleepless nights this book would have been finished much earlier. I hope you and all children who come from a country of conflict don't let it color who you are. It's indescribable how much Mama loves you.

—N. K.

BLOOMSBURY CHILDREN'S BOOKS
Bloomsbury Publishing Inc., part of Bloomsbury Publishing Plc
1385 Broadway, New York, NY 10018

BLOOMSBURY, BLOOMSBURY CHILDREN'S BOOKS, and the Diana logo are trademarks of Bloomsbury Publishing Plc

First published in the United States of America in November 2020
by Bloomsbury Children's Books

Bloomsbury books may be purchased for business or promotional use. For information on bulk
purchases please contact Macmillan Corporate and Premium Sales Department at specialmarkets@macmillan.com

Library of Congress Cataloging-in-Publication Data
Names: Fakher, Bassel Abou, author. | Blumenthal, Deborah, author. | Kaadan, Nadine, illustrator.
Title: Saving Stella / by Bassel Abou Fakher and Deborah Blumenthal ; illustrated by Nadine Kaadan.
Description: New York : Bloomsbury Children's Books, 2020.
Summary: A musician and his dog escape war-torn Syria.
Identifiers: LCCN 2020012724 (print) | LCCN 2020012725 (e-book)
ISBN 978-1-5476-0133-2 (hardcover) • ISBN 978-1-5476-0134-9 (e-book) • ISBN 978-1-5476-0135-6 (e-PDF)
Subjects: LCSH: Dogs—Syria—Juvenile literature. | Human-animal relationships—Juvenile literature. | Syria—History—Civil War,
2011—Personal narratives—Juvenile literature. | Syria—History—Civil War, 2011—Refugees—Juvenile literature.
Classification: LCC SF426.5 .F35 2020 (print) | LCC SF426.5 (e-book) | DDC 636.7—dc23
LC record available at https://lccn.loc.gov/2020012724
LC e-book record available at https://lccn.loc.gov/2020012725

Art rendered with watercolors and colored pencils
Typeset in Warnock Pro
Book design by Danielle Ceccolini
Printed in China by Leo Paper Products, Heshan, Guangdong
2 4 6 8 10 9 7 5 3 1

All papers used by Bloomsbury Publishing Plc are natural, recyclable products made
from wood grown in well-managed forests. The manufacturing processes conform
to the environmental regulations of the country of origin.

To find out more about our authors and books visit www.bloomsbury.com and sign up for our newsletters.

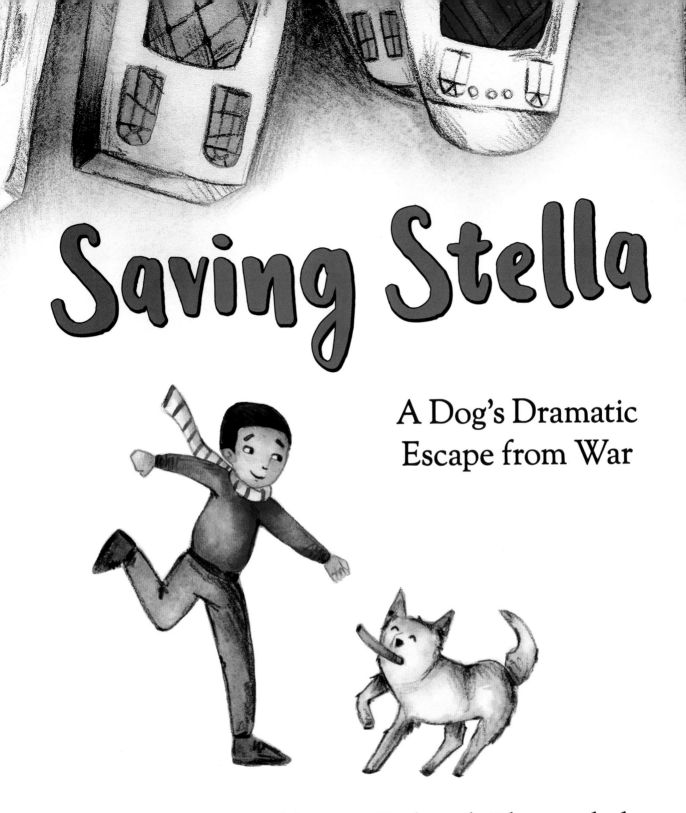

Saving Stella

A Dog's Dramatic Escape from War

Bassel Abou Fakher AND Deborah Blumenthal

ILLUSTRATED BY Nadine Kaadan

BLOOMSBURY
CHILDREN'S BOOKS
NEW YORK LONDON OXFORD NEW DELHI SYDNEY

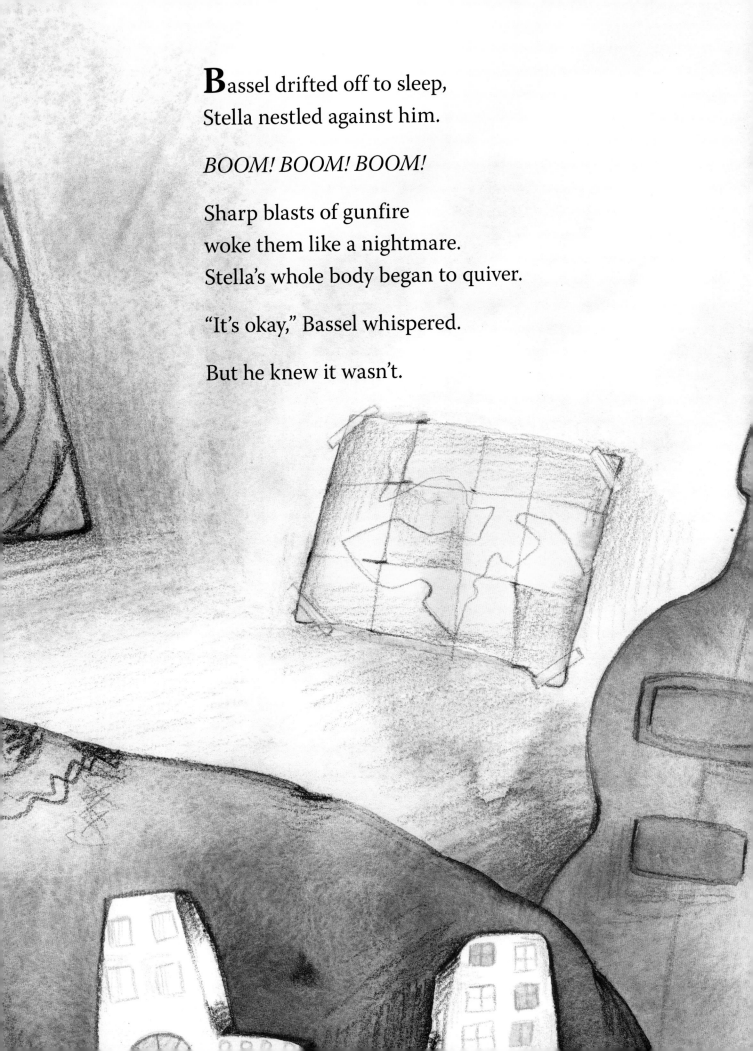

Bassel drifted off to sleep,
Stella nestled against him.

BOOM! BOOM! BOOM!

Sharp blasts of gunfire
woke them like a nightmare.
Stella's whole body began to quiver.

"It's okay," Bassel whispered.

But he knew it wasn't.

Even in his own bed he wasn't safe,
because home was
in Damascus, a city
in a country called Syria,
where war was raging.

Rebel groups wanted a new leader,
but the president refused to leave.

The year was 2015.

The fighting grew wider.
Gunfire and explosives ripped through the city.
Bombs toppled buildings like wooden blocks.
Parents were afraid to go out to buy food.
Children were afraid to go to school.

Still, dogs had to be walked,
so Bassel led Stella around the block.
Step
by
step,
pretending it was okay.

The war went on and on.
Bassel, a musician,
couldn't live in a city that was collapsing.
He had to escape.

But that meant saying goodbye,
to family,
to friends.

And to Stella.

The trip was too hard for a dog.
She would have to stay
behind with his parents.

Bassel had no choice.

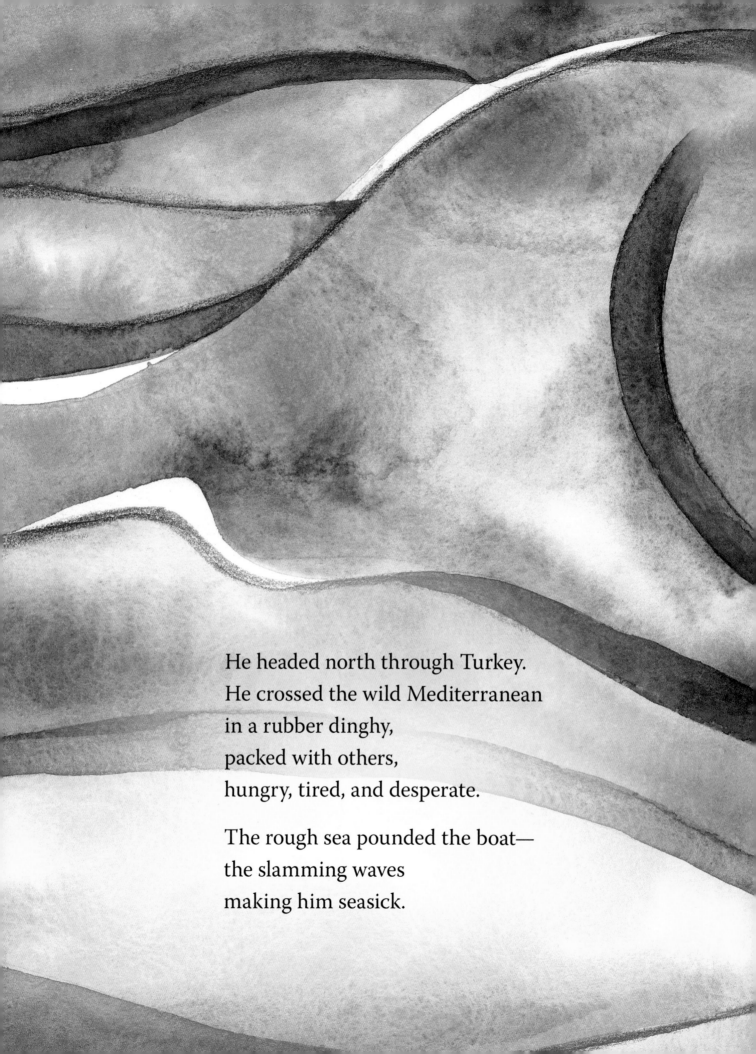

He headed north through Turkey.
He crossed the wild Mediterranean
in a rubber dinghy,
packed with others,
hungry, tired, and desperate.

The rough sea pounded the boat—
the slamming waves
making him seasick.

Many hours later they reached land.
But he still wasn't free.
He was held in a refugee camp
like a prisoner.

But Bassel was lucky.
Almost two months later,
he left.

He found a safe place to live in Brussels, Belgium,
with Joannes, a man with a family
whose heart went out to those fleeing war.

Stella wasn't so lucky.

Bassel spoke to family back in Damascus
and learned that Stella wasn't being walked anymore.
She lived on greasy food scraps and gained weight.
Worst of all,
day and night she
had to endure the deafening
sounds of war.

Bassel had taken risks to save himself.
Now he had to try to save Stella.

Bassel told Joannes about Stella,
and they hatched a plan.

A taxi driver they knew
back in Syria
named Rasheed
would fetch Stella
and drive her to Beirut, Lebanon.
In Beirut, Joannes and Bassel's friend Fares
would take Stella.
Then Joannes would fly to Brussels
with Stella.

There was a good chance guards
would stop Rasheed at the border
and send him back.

But if it worked, Stella would come home to Bassel.

Rasheed put Stella in his car.
His taxi was stopped at checkpoint after checkpoint
on the road from Damascus to Beirut.

"Where are you going?"
men with guns asked him again and again.
"Why do you have that dog with you?"

Dangerous gangs lurked on the roadside.
Would someone jump out at him?
Would he be pulled from his car and held prisoner?

After hours on the road,
they crossed the border safely into Lebanon.

Fares met them and lifted Stella
from the car.
Her bright eyes
were now clouded with fear.

Fares and Joannes took Stella to a local veterinarian
for the papers she needed to fly.

But then at the airport they realized
they didn't have the pill to keep her calm.
Joannes rushed back to the veterinarian.

Joannes and Fares
struggled to put Stella into a crate,
but it wasn't easy.
She didn't want to go.
She didn't want to take the pill.

And all the while,
the police were watching.

Joannes got Stella onto the plane.
Her crate was put deep inside the cargo hold.

Fares started to leave the airport,
but the police grabbed him and took him to the station.
Who would go to so much trouble for a dog during wartime?
It looked suspicious to them.
After hours of questioning,
they finally released him.

Meanwhile, Bassel waited at the airport in Brussels.
Where was she?
Was she safe?
Did she make it?

When the plane landed,
Bassel waited as the luggage
and the cargo were unloaded.

Then he saw the crate.

There was Stella,
eyes wide, watching.
She stared at Bassel through the bars,
and he stared back at her.

They had been separated for nearly eight months,
and she didn't seem to recognize him.

But dogs remember,
even though sometimes
the memories
seem hidden inside.

Now, in Brussels,
Stella has a new, safe home.
She has grown fit and strong again
from running outside in a lush garden.
And her new home has a balcony
where she can bask in the sunlight,
like a tulip in spring,
all the bright new days
overshadowing the dark ones.

Like Bassel,
Stella has two lives.
Then.
And now.

One is lost.
And one is found.

A Note from Bassel

Photo courtesy of Bassel Abou Fakher

We knew we would have to leave Syria. There were car bombings, kidnappings, and violence in the streets. Everyone was afraid to go outside. We tried to go to the United Arab Emirates, where my uncle lived, to see if we could get visas, but that didn't work out. We looked into going to Europe too, but weren't able to.

So the family separated. I was nineteen when I left on August 30, 2015. My girlfriend and three friends went with me. We left with others in a rubber raft. I didn't bring food because there was no space for it. All I had was my laptop, my hard drive, and fifty CDs, all filled with my own music.

It was a five-and-a-half-hour trip on the open water, and I was dizzy and nauseous. I went from Turkey to Greece and then by train and by walking to Austria and then Belgium. There I was held in a refugee camp near a city called Hasselt. After about two months, I left.

I was one of the lucky ones. I made my way to Brussels, where I met people who helped me, particularly a man named Joannes and his family, who opened their home and their hearts to me. My parents and older sister, Yara, are now in different parts of the world, and Joannes, his wife, Ann, their daughters, Martha and Helene, and their son, Jozef, have become my new family.

After six months, it was time to have Stella brought out so she could have a peaceful and happy life too. Joannes welcomed her the way he welcomed me. Stella was very stressed after she got here. While she's getting better, if she sees Belgian soldiers in uniform, she gets super traumatized. They remind her of the soldiers in Syria.

My life and my work here are centered around music, which is my passion. I am very motivated, trying to learn all sides of it. It's an endless thing, I know, but it's what I love.

Will I go back to Syria? I don't think so. Home for me is where I feel safe and where I can make my future memories with people I care about. This city has been kind enough to me to make me feel at home.

A Note from Nadine

I was born in France, but I lived in Syria all my life until 2012, when I was twenty-seven. I left because staying safe had become too difficult for me and my family. I was convinced that it would be for only six months, until things settled down—six months became twelve months, which became eight years and counting. But I'm much more fortunate than most. I'm still able to visit home from time to time to see family and friends. I also didn't have to risk treacherous seas and poisonous politics to find a peaceful shore; I was able to just book a flight to London and leave. I often think of Bassel's journey, and I am deeply moved and distressed by it in equal measure because I know that so many didn't make it. I always find it difficult to understand how a small document such as a passport can sometimes define our humanity.

I am really happy that Bassel and Stella were reunited at the end. Sadly, I lost my beloved cat, Jarour, when a bomb struck our Damascus neighborhood in 2013. Jarour continues to be a source of inspiration in my stories and a part of my memories of home.

When the war started, my work changed completely. My normally bright illustrations became darker, and the shock of my country tearing itself apart was immediately reflected in my stories. The once-dreamy colors and tales inspired by the magical architecture of Damascus were slowly replaced by drawings of destroyed buildings and devastated lives. My focus now is to represent my country's indomitable resilience—something I find particularly important during a time of naked prejudice, misrepresentation, and travel bans.

Visiting refugee camps and Syrian diaspora communities and reading my books to children has been a source of hope and inspiration for me. I do my best to try to help kids make some sense of the overwhelming nature of war. More important, I try to keep reminding them (and myself) that we cannot allow a temporary brutal conflict to color who we are or to make us forget the beauty of where we come from.

More about the Syrian War and the Worldwide Refugee Crisis

Imagine not having a home or a bed to sleep in. Imagine not having shelter from frigid winters and sweltering summers. Imagine being so hungry that your belly hurts from not having enough to eat.

About twenty-five million children, women, and men don't have to imagine this. They had to flee from Syria, a country in the Middle East, and from other countries around the world. They are refugees: people forced to leave their homelands because of war and violence on their doorsteps. Every day of their lives, refugees face hardship and uncertainty.

International law is supposed to protect people facing human tragedy, but the countries of the world who should be working together are not.

THE MIDDLE EAST

Courtesy of PSboom/Shutterstock.com

The turmoil in Syria began building in 2011. The president, Bashar al-Assad, has been in power since 2000. Before him, the country was led by his father. Different rebel groups, who have different ideas about how the country should be run, have attempted to remove Assad from office. But the Syrian president's military is strong, and he is backed by other larger, powerful countries such as Russia, Iran, and Turkey. The United States once supported the Kurds, one of the largest rebel groups, but it no longer does.

Assad has managed to fight off those who oppose him, but the war has lasted for nine years and still continues. It has devastated the country. It is no longer safe to go to school or to go outside and play. If you are sick, it is hard to get to a doctor. Homes are often dark because there is no electricity.

All the fighting between the government and the rebel groups has led to a war that has taken a terrible toll on the peaceful citizens of Syria. As of 2016, the United Nations and the Arab League envoy to Syria estimated that 400,000 people had been killed in the war. As of 2019, the figure was closer to 500,000, and the killings go on.

More than half of the almost 25 million people living in Syria before the war have been forced to leave their homes, moving to other parts of the country or to other countries. And it's not just a crisis for people. Many, many pets were abandoned and lost their lives because their owners fled to safety and were unable to take them. Others wander the streets without food or shelter, a heartbreaking sight for animal lovers who think of their dogs and cats as members of their families.

But if you are a refugee, finding another country willing to offer you asylum permanently isn't easy.

While most refugees come from Africa, the Middle East, and South Asia, there is political upheaval all over the globe, and the numbers of those needing help are greater than ever.

Unfortunately, the number of people allowed to enter safer countries is far smaller than the numbers who need help. Some countries fear refugees because they follow a different faith or have different cultural practices. Others imagine that refugees will take away their jobs. Some countries have placed strict limits on the numbers of people they allow in because of the cost and the difficulty of finding new homes for refugees and then helping them adjust to their new lives.

There are no easy answers for people who are forced to leave their countries because they fear for their safety.

What is important to remember is that refugees are people just like us. They deserve our respect, sympathy, and whatever help we can offer them. In addition, countries need to join together to forge stronger bonds to help people in crisis as soon as war, famine, pandemics, devastating weather, or other catastrophic events threaten their well-being.

What can you do? Donate clothes and toys to groups that aid refugees. Donate money if you can afford to do so. If you meet someone in your community who has arrived to start over, welcome them, especially new students in your school. It's always hard for people to feel comfortable in new surroundings, so be friendly and helpful. When it's time to vote, urge your parents to cast their ballots for candidates who support assisting refugees around the globe, not politicians who turn their backs on them.

More than half the refugees in the world are children, just like you.

For More Information

https://www.parents.com/parents-magazine/parents-perspective/talking-to-kids-about-the
   -refugee-crisis/

https://www.savethechildren.org/us/what-we-do/emergency-response/refugee-children-crisis
   /what-is-refugee

https://www.unicefusa.org/mission/emergencies/child-refugees